MW01629321

Prompt Me Novel

Fiction Writing Journal & Workbook

Prompt Me Series #6

By

Robin Woods

Epic Books Publishing

Lead editor: Beth Braithwaite
Other editing: Tamar Hela

Cover Design created on Canva by Robin Woods

Fonts: Century, Arial, Ariel Unicode

Summary: A writing workbook that offers guidance and resources for organizing a fiction novel.

[Non-Fiction, Writing Workbook, Fiction Writing, Writing Journal, Writing Reference]

ISBN-13: 978-1-941077-16-0
ISBN-10: 1-941077-16-1

Originally published as: *Fiction Writing Workbook & Journal*

Table of Contents

Foreword

By Tamar Hela

In an age where we rely more and more on technology, it is imperative to preserve the act and art of writing by hand. Studies show that our brains process information in a different way when we use pen and paper. Some research even suggests that using the mighty pen boosts memory and the ability to not only retain concepts, but to understand them.

This workbook provides a space for you to journal ideas and thoughts for your next–or first–best seller. Robin not only shares her knowledge gained by years of experience, but thoughtfully gives space for writers to reflect and hand-write their ideas and moments of inspiration.

As a writer, professional editor, and Language Arts teacher, I can't stress enough what a gift this workbook is. So, I encourage you–take advantage of every piece of advice and of every page where you can write and be inspired. Discover a new technique or reconnect with an old method. However you write and however you plan your novel, know that expert help is right here at your fingertips.

Happy writing!

Introduction

"There is nothing to writing. All you do is sit down at a typewriter and bleed."

— Ernest Hemingway

Writing is an art, but it takes perseverance more than anything. After writing half a dozen novels and reading hundreds of articles on writing, one truth rises to the top—actually sitting down and getting words on the page is the biggest obstacle. So, my number one piece of advice? Make writing a daily *habit.* This can be for a set time, like one hour, or a word count goal, like 5,000 words a day. You are the one who sets your goal—set reasonable goals and do it.

Many books will give you an overly structured approach to writing, but that is not the intent of this workbook/journal. My goals are to give you the basic structure and powerful resources to help you reach your goal. To me, overly structured often equals overly formulaic. Don't get me wrong; you need some formula. There should be a beginning, middle, and an end—and of course, an inciting incident followed by rising action and eventually, a climax. There should also be a large amount of conflict, because without conflict, there is no story. But your writing should likewise be inspired and have twists that no one sees coming. Set up your audience to believe that you are heading in one direction, and then come at them from another side.

When I am working on a novel, I picture it like a messy workshop. With the first draft, I write quickly, giving myself space to make mistakes, not worrying about the technical elements as much. The most important aspect is to get the words on the page. Rough is just fine. Then, I go back with the honing tools, where I chisel and reshape. Eventually, I get to the technical finish work before sending it to my editors (yes, plural) and beta readers.

Do not stress about being perfect on your first draft—simply get it done. This workbook will walk you through story structure, developmental exercises, and improvement suggestions and provide charts for efficiency.

Before diving in, thumb through the resources in the back; they will help you avoid some common mistakes and supply you with new ideas.

Now, go forth and write.

Plot

Plot Structures

Before forging ahead, it would be a good idea to look over some established tropes. The most basic formats are stories with a happy, sad, or bitter-sweet ending. When researching the topic, scholars group plot archetypes into anything from seven to thirty-six categories. The debate comes down to whether it is important to study these structures. The answer: At minimum, look into the archetype that you choose for your story. Not only will it give you a key to marketing your book in the future, but it will allow you to play with classic storylines and turn those plots on their head.

Plot Archetypes	
Adventure	Hero travels to a different land > encounters trials > returns with only experience as treasure
	The Hobbit, The Time Machine, Alice's Adventures in Wonderland, Chronicles of Narnia
Boy Meets Girl	Boy meets girl > boy loses girl > boy wins girl back (some variations have a tragic twist ending)
	Pride & Prejudice, Austenland, Tess of the D'Urbervilles, When Harry Met Sally, The Great Gatsby, The Notebook
Comedy	Light and humorous > happy ending
	Much Ado About Nothing, Midsummer Night's Dream, Twelfth Night, Zoolander
Coming of Age	Innocent exposed to the real world > grows
	Candide, The Day No Pigs Would Die, The Yearling, American Graffiti, Stand by Me
Golem Stories	Something created to serve > creation rises to destroy the creator
	Frankenstein, Pygmalion, Prometheus, The Terminator, The X Files "Kaddish," *Sleepy Hollow* "Golem"
Good Versus Evil	Hero is called to defeat a monster > encounters trials > triumphs when all looks to be lost
	Beowulf, David and Goliath, Dracula, Lord of the Rings, War of the Worlds, Jack & the Beanstalk, Star Wars, Alien
Rags to Riches	Protagonist is low on social scale > gains something of value > loses everything > grows as a person > rewarded
	Cinderella, Jane Eyre, Oliver Twist, Rocky , Great Expectations, Pretty Woman, Aladdin, My Fair Lady

<table>
<tr><td rowspan="2">Rebirth</td><td>A flawed person > event changes them > rewarded</td></tr>
<tr><td>Beauty & the Beast, A Christmas Carol, The Secret Garden, The Shawshank Redemption, Despicable Me</td></tr>
<tr><td rowspan="2">Star-Crossed Lovers</td><td>Boy meets girl > love causes destruction of selves or world</td></tr>
<tr><td>Romeo & Juliet, Wuthering Heights, Tristan & Isolde, Trollies & Cressida, Buffy the Vampire Slayer (Buffy and Angel)</td></tr>
<tr><td rowspan="2">The Fall</td><td>From Aristotle's Poetics: Respected figure > hero's error or tragic flaw > reversal of fortune > recognition > suffering > resolution and catharsis (death is the happy ending)</td></tr>
<tr><td>Macbeth, Julius Caesar, Oedipus, Dr. Faustus, Hamlet, King Lear, Othello, Hedda Gabler, Breaking Bad</td></tr>
<tr><td rowspan="2">The Quest</td><td>The hero (often with friends) > seeks object or location > encounters trials on the journey</td></tr>
<tr><td>Iliad, Odyssey, Star Wars, Shrek, Indiana Jones</td></tr>
<tr><td rowspan="2">Revenge</td><td>The protagonist is wronged > plots revenge</td></tr>
<tr><td>The Count of Monte Cristo, Hamlet, Moby Dick, Carrie, "The Cask of Amontillado," Inigo in The Princess Bride, Death Wish, Gladiator</td></tr>
<tr><td rowspan="2">Mystery</td><td>Crime is perpetrated > investigator takes up quest to solve</td></tr>
<tr><td>Sherlock Holmes, Agatha Christie novels, Castle, crime shows</td></tr>
</table>

Other Notes on Plot Structure:

Brainstorming

Visually lay out your ideas and connect the coordinating thoughts. I know, I know: you just want to jump in. Trust me, taking a little time to explore can make your writing sparkle later.

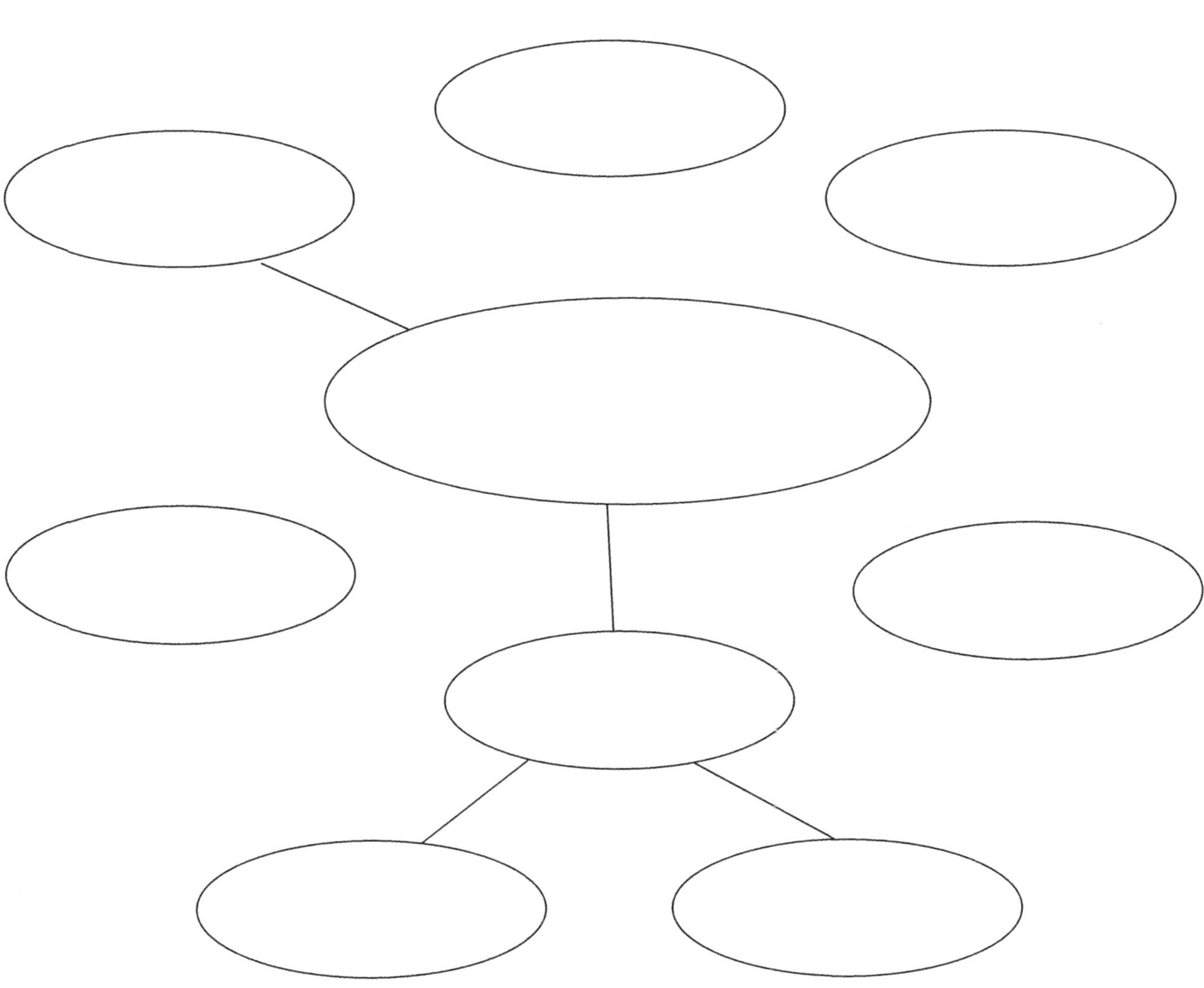

More Brainstorming

Simple Outline

Don't get bogged down in the details yet. Create a general outline with the major movements of your piece. *Note: If you are going to query an agent or a publishing company, you will need a full outline.*

I. ______________________________

A.

B.

II. ______________________________

A.

B.

III. ______________________________

A.

B.

IV. ______________________________

A.

B.

V. ______________________________

A.

B.

Other Plot Points

Tent Poles

Now that you have the general course of your novel plotted, think about the scenes with the most conflict. I usually write those three or four sections before I do anything else. These are my "tent pole" scenes. These are the game changers that carry emotional weight. Knowing where you are headed is imperative. Once you have those scenes locked in, think of the rest of the process as connecting the dots.

Spend a few minutes outlining or writing your game changers:

Tagline, Summary, and Blurb

A tagline is a single phrase or sentence catchphrase used in advertising. Keep it clear and simple, and leave the audience wanting more. You don't need to do this now, but if you are inspired, keep a list. There is room on the next page for brainstorming.

Tagline:

Sample taglines from the movies: *Jaws,* "Don't go in the water;" *Catch Me If You Can*, "The true story of a real fake;" *Erin Brockovich,* "She brought a small town to its feet and a huge corporation to its knees;" *Lord of the Rings,* "One ring to rule them all;" and *Alien,* "In space, no one can hear you scream."

This description is a synopsis of the main events in the novel. Make sure you don't ruin a plotline. Less is more.

Summary:

A blurb is the description you find on the back of a book. It is written from a marketing point of view with the intention of selling the work. It should be no more than three paragraphs.

Blurb:

Plot Diagram

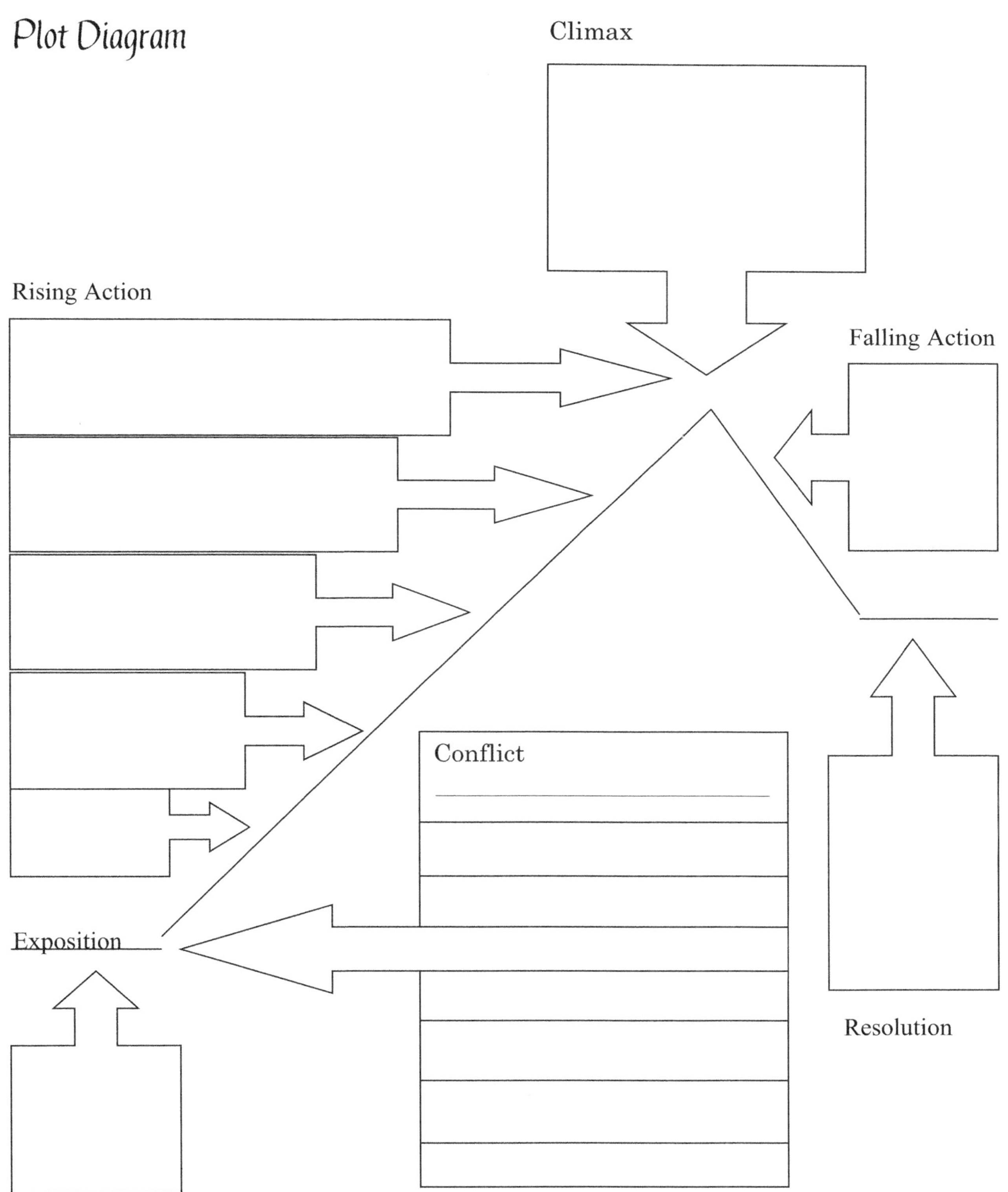

Thoughts and Notes on Plot

Plot Assignment

All writers need to be readers. Stephen King says, "If you don't have time to read, you don't have the time (or the tools) to write. Simple as that." Keeping that in mind, pick a best-selling novel in your genre. Read it, but read it as a writer, and do the following:

- Make a brief outline of the plot as you go.
- Pay attention to the pacing.
- Chart the average chapter length.
- Note how much description the author includes.
- Ask: How often is a new conflict added?

Name of Novel ____ Author ____________________

Genre _____________________________ Number of Pages ______ Number of Chapters ______

Average Chapter Length __________

Basic Outline of the Novel

Chapter One

Number of Pages _____

Opening line:

How does the author introduce the setting?

Characters:

Events:

Other notes:

Chapter Two

Number of Pages _____

How does the author introduce the conflict?

Characters:

Events:

Other notes:

The story should be rolling by now. Keep track of the conflicts, plots, and unique characteristics.

Chapter Three

Number of Pages _____

Conflicts & Events:

Other notes:

Chapter Four

Number of Pages _____

Conflicts & Events:

Other notes:

Chapter Five

Number of Pages _____

Conflicts & Events:

Other notes:

Chapter Six

Number of Pages _____

Conflicts & Events:

Other notes:

Chapter Seven

Number of Pages _____

Conflicts & Events:

Other notes:

Chapter Eight

Number of Pages _____

Conflicts & Events:

Other notes:

Chapter Nine

Number of Pages _____

Conflicts & Events:

Other notes:

Chapter Ten

Number of Pages _____

Conflicts & Events:

Other notes:

Chapter Eleven

Number of Pages _____

Conflicts & Events:

Other notes:

Chapter Twelve

Number of Pages _____

Conflicts & Events:

Other notes:

Chapter Thirteen

Number of Pages _____

Conflicts & Events:

Other notes:

Chapter Fourteen

Number of Pages _____

Conflicts & Events:

Other notes:

Chapter Fifteen

Number of Pages _____

Conflicts & Events:

Other notes:

Chapter Sixteen

Number of Pages _____

Conflicts & Events:

Other notes:

Book Analysis Continued:

Conflict

Conflict Is Key

Without conflict, there is no plot. The largest conflict should be introduced in the rising action, and remember, conflict is more than just a fight.

Basic Types of Conflict	**Example**
Person vs. Person	*Lord of the Flies, Othello,* "The Cask of Amontillado," "The Most Dangerous Game"
Person vs. Nature	*Moby Dick, Old Man and the Sea,* "To Build a Fire," Any disaster book or film
Person vs. Society	*To Kill a Mockingbird, Catcher in the Rye, The Giver, 1984, The Scarlet Letter, Fahrenheit 451, Hunger Games*
Person vs. Him or Herself	*Hamlet, Dr. Faustus, Death of a Salesman, The Bridget Jones Diary*
Person vs. Fate	Odyssey, *Oedipus Rex, Slaughterhouse Five*
Person vs. the Supernatural	*Dr. Jekyll and Mr. Hyde,* "The Monkey's Paw," The Shining, Any zombie book or film
Person vs. Technology	*The Terminator, The Matrix*

Is the conflict about: value systems, relationships, history, interests, information, structures, psychology, self-esteem, skills, experiences, styles, power, legacy, reputation?

Think About:

What types of conflict do you plan to include?

What is going to make your conflict different?

What is the cause of the conflict? Is it realistic or petty?

Is the conflict surface, latent (dormant or concealed), or open?

Do some brainstorming on the next few pages:

Setting

Setting as Painted by the Masters

Writers need to read, read, read—pick both classics and books in your chosen genre. Here are some fantastic examples of setting and exposition.

Harper Lee's description of Maycomb from *To Kill a Mockingbird*

Maycomb was an old town, but it was a tired old town when I first knew it. In rainy weather the streets turned to red slop; grass grew on the sidewalks, the courthouse sagged in the square. Somehow, it was hotter then: a black dog suffered on a summer's day; bony mules hitched to Hoover carts flicked flies in the sweltering shade of the live oaks on the square. Men's stiff collars wilted by nine in the morning. Ladies bathed before noon, after their three-o'clock naps, and by nightfall were like soft teacakes with frostings of sweat and sweet talcum. People moved slowly then. They ambled across the square, shuffled in and out of the stores around it, took their time about everything. A day was twenty-four hours long but seemed longer. There was no hurry, for there was nowhere to go, nothing to buy and no money to buy it with, nothing to see outside the boundaries of Maycomb County…

Lee not only gives a solid description of the town, but infuses it with attitude and feeling as well.

Charlotte Perkins Gilman from "The Yellow Wallpaper"

It is a big, airy room, the whole floor nearly, with windows that look all ways, and air and sunshine galore. It was nursery first and then playroom… I should judge; for the windows are barred for little children, and there are rings and things in the walls. The paint and paper look as if a boys' school had used it. It is stripped off—the paper—in great patches all around the head of my bed, about as far as I can reach, and in a great place on the other side of the room low down.

I never saw a worse paper in my life. One of those sprawling flamboyant patterns committing every artistic sin. It is dull enough to confuse the eye in following, pronounced enough to constantly irritate and provoke study, and when you follow the lame uncertain curves for a little distance they suddenly commit suicide—plunge off at outrageous angles, destroy themselves in unheard of contradictions. The color is repellent, almost revolting; a smouldering unclean yellow, strangely faded by the slow-turning sunlight. It is a dull yet lurid orange in some places, a sickly sulphur tint in others. No wonder the children hated it! I should hate it myself if I had to live in this room long.

Gilman takes the time to describe the wallpaper because it becomes a character in the story.

Franz Kafka from "The Metamorphosis"

His room, a proper human room although a little too small, lay peacefully between its four familiar walls. A collection of textile samples lay spread out on the table—Samsa was a travelling salesman—and above it there hung a picture that he had recently cut out of an illustrated magazine and housed in a nice, gilded frame. It showed a lady fitted out with a fur hat and fur boa who sat upright, raising a heavy fur muff that covered the whole of her lower arm towards the viewer.

Kafka not only describes the surroundings, but manages to include indirect characterization of Samsa.

A Look Deeper

What works in the examples on the previous page?

List some of the visual words that the authors use:

Do they only use sight words? Or, do they tap into more of the senses?

Look at the point of view. Two are from first person and one from third person. How does this choice help or detract from the narrative?

Additional Notes:

Exposition and Setting

The setting you introduce in the first two chapters will set the tone for the entire novel (and/or series). Take the time to craft it correctly. Describe it in as much detail as you want in your first draft, being careful not to over edit as you write. You may come up with some wonderful description that can be used elsewhere. In your second (or even tenth) draft, streamline, taking flow and pacing into account—wordy is fine in the creation stage, so go for it.

Questions to consider: (Do some brainstorming here.)

What does your world look like?

What does your world *feel* like? Come up with a list of adjectives that you can refer to later.

How does the setting impact the plot?

How does the world impact your characters?

Is the setting a character in itself?

Are you going to focus on a wide spectrum or on smaller details? Sometimes it helps to visualize the introduction as a film. Are there going to be sweeping visuals and close-ups?

Go back to one of your favorite books and re-read the first chapter. How does the author introduce the setting? Take notes on the items you like and don't like.

Introducing Setting

There are different ways to go about the introductory exposition, but broken into their simplest elements, there are two:

1. Introduce your setting, and then the main character in that world.

2. Reveal the character first, then obviously, the setting.

Below are two examples from classic short stories. They both introduce the setting and characters in a different order. Since they are from older literature, the language is a bit more difficult, but the structure is what we are looking at. Start noting the technical elements when you read. I have marked point of view and verb tense.

Point of View: First
Verb Tense: Past
"The Cask of Amontillado" by Edgar Allan Poe

In the short story sample below, the writer spends time developing the protagonist and his motivations before describing the setting.

The thousand injuries of Fortunato I had borne as I best could, but when he ventured upon insult, I vowed revenge. You, who so well know the nature of my soul, will not suppose, however, that I gave utterance to a threat. *At length* I would be avenged; this was a point definitely settled—but the very definitiveness with which it was resolved, precluded the idea of risk. I must not only punish, but punish with impunity. A wrong is unredressed when retribution overtakes its redresser. It is equally unredressed when the avenger fails to make himself felt as such to him who has done the wrong.

It must be understood that neither by word nor deed had I given Fortunato cause to doubt my good will. I continued, as was my wont, to smile in his face, and he did not perceive that my smile *now* was at the thought of his immolation.

He had a weak point—this Fortunato—although in other regards he was a man to be respected and even feared. He prided himself on his connoisseurship in wine. Few Italians have the true virtuoso spirit. For the most part their enthusiasm is adopted to suit the time and opportunity—to practise imposture upon the British and Austrian *millionaires*. In painting and gemmary, Fortunato, like his countrymen, was a quack—but in the matter of old wines he was sincere. In this respect I did not differ from him materially: I was skillful in the Italian vintages myself, and bought largely whenever I could.

It was about dusk, one evening during the supreme madness of the carnival season, that I encountered my friend. He accosted me with excessive warmth, for he had been drinking much. The man wore motley. He had on a tight-fitting parti-striped dress, and his head was surmounted by the conical cap and bells. I was so pleased to see him, that I thought I should never have done wringing his hand.

Point of View: Third Person
Verb Tense: Past
"An Occurrence at Owl Creek Bridge" by Ambrose Bierce

In this excerpt, the author maps the setting, carefully plotting where each character is standing, since it is significant to the story. The tale takes place during the American Civil War. Though not in this sample, this story is also a great example of a non-linear timeline. Bierce was ahead of his time, as modern writers often imitate the format he was using in the 1890s.

A man stood upon a railroad bridge in northern Alabama, looking down into the swift water twenty feet below. The man's hands were behind his back, the wrists bound with a cord. A rope closely encircled his neck. It was attached to a stout cross-timber above his head and the slack fell to the level of his knees. Some loose boards laid upon the ties supporting the rails of the railway supplied a footing for him and his executioners—two private soldiers of the Federal army, directed by a sergeant who in civil life may have been a deputy sheriff. At a short remove upon the same temporary platform was an officer in the uniform of his rank, armed. He was a captain. A sentinel at each end of the bridge stood with his rifle in the position known as "support," that is to say, vertical in front of the left shoulder, the hammer resting on the forearm thrown straight across the chest—a formal and unnatural position, enforcing an erect carriage of the body. It did not appear to be the duty of these two men to know what was occurring at the center of the bridge; they merely blockaded the two ends of the foot planking that traversed it.

Beyond one of the sentinels nobody was in sight; the railroad ran straight away into a forest for a hundred yards, then, curving, was lost to view. Doubtless there was an outpost farther along. The other bank of the stream was open ground—a gentle slope topped with a stockade of vertical tree trunks, loopholed for rifles, with a single embrasure through which protruded the muzzle of a brass cannon commanding the bridge. Midway up the slope between the bridge and fort were the spectators—a single company of infantry in line, at "parade rest," the butts of their rifles on the ground, the barrels inclining slightly backward against the right shoulder, the hands crossed upon the stock. A lieutenant stood at the right of the line, the point of his sword upon the ground, his left hand resting upon his right. Excepting the group of four at the center of the bridge, not a man moved. The company faced the bridge, staring stonily, motionless. The sentinels, facing the banks of the stream, might have been statues to adorn the bridge. The captain stood with folded arms, silent, observing the work of his subordinates, but making no sign. Death is a dignitary who when he comes announced is to be received with formal manifestations of respect, even by those most familiar with him. In the code of military etiquette silence and fixity are forms of deference.

What does and doesn't work for you in these samples?

Write two introductory paragraphs:

1. Introduce the character, then the setting.

2. Begin with the setting, and then the character.

Points of View

Points of View

Decide what point of view best fits your writing style and your project. I prefer a limited perspective, be it first or third. Why? Keeping secrets from your audience can be a powerful tool. You can write from more than one perspective, but you need to be clear. Otherwise, you risk fracturing the narrative of the novel, making it too hard to follow. So, no switching POV in the middle of a scene.

☐ **First Person**
Emotional Standpoint: Subjective
View: Limited
Pronoun Usage: I/we/us/me/mine/our/ours

☐ **Third Person Limited**
Emotional Standpoint: Objective
View: Limited
Pronoun Usage: he/she/it/his/her/they/their

☐ **Third Person Omniscient** (Not Recommended for New Writers)
Emotional Standpoint: Objective
View: Unlimited
Pronoun Usage: he/she/it/his/her/they/their

☐ **Deep Third Person**
Emotional Standpoint: Subjective
View: Limited
Pronoun Usage: he/she/it/his/her/they/their

If you aren't sure which to choose, it might be wise to chart the pros and cons of a specific style. The most popular styles are first and third person.

PROs and CONs	

Now that you have thought about point of view, write a paragraph from two different perspectives and see which one is more natural for you.

Character

Character Archetypes

The American Heritage Dictionary defines a stock character as: "(noun) character in literature, theatre, or film of a type quickly recognized and accepted by the reader or viewer and requiring no development by the writer." One of the beauties of this type of character is that archetypes cannot be copyrighted. You are free to use any of them without worrying.

Your protagonist and antagonist are usually an amalgam of many character archetypes. The supporting characters tend to function in one of these capacities: the sidekick, love interest, mentor, fool, or nemesis.

If you want your characters to have depth, it is often good to start with an archetype, and then add other characteristics to that character.

Sample Character Archetypes		
Academic	Flatterer (Sycophant)	Politician
Anti-hero	Foil	Priest
Athlete	Fool	Rebel
Bad Boy	Genius	Red Shirt (Cannon Fodder)
Battle Axe	Guardian	Ruler
Black Knight	Hero	Scapegoat (Fall guy)
Caregiver	Innocent Youth (Ingénue)	Seer
Christ Figure	Jester	Shrew
Courtesan	Loner	Sidekick
Creator	Love Interest	Spoiled Child
Crone	Magician	Temptress
Damsel in Distress	Malcontent	Tomboy
Destroyer	Mentor	Trickster
Dirty Old Man	Miser (Scrooge)	Unwilling Hero
Doppelgänger	Mother Figure	Villain
Explorer	Nemesis	Warrior
Everyman (Commoner)	Old Man	White Knight
Father Figure	Orphan	Wise Elder
Femme Fatale	Outlaw	Young Lover
Other Archetypes:		

Naming Characters

Naming characters can be a difficult task. Sometimes they just come to me, and other times, I search and claw and bang my head against the keyboard (figuratively, at least). I want the name to not only *feel* and *sound* right, but also to convey some sort of meaning, at least, most of the time. I have been guilty of trolling name site for so long, I use up all of my writing time (I would never procrastinate).

A few tips:

- **Vary the length of the names you pick.** Not every character should have a three-syllable name. I have put down more than one fantasy novel because all of the names were ridiculously long and complicated. Don't do it—even Tolkien had a character named Sam.
- **Consider nicknames when you are deciding**. Make it easier on your reader and offer a few shorter names. Just make sure they are catchy.
- **Have a healthy balance of regular and unique names.**
- **I have compiled all of my favorite name databases and generators in one blog post** and keep it regularly updated. If you are interested in checking it out, simply scan the QR code below or go to my website and type "naming" into the search bar.

www.RobinWoodsFiction.com

Go to my blog:

Writing Resource: What's in a Name?

http://robinwoodsfiction.com/2015/01/20/writing-resource-whats-in-a-name/

Character Name Research

Character Lists

As you go, keep a running list of all of the characters and their descriptions in the manuscript.

Protagonist:

Antagonist:

Protagonist Family:

Antagonist Family:

Protagonist Friends:

Antagonist Friends:

Other Characters:

Names I Find Appealing

As you research names, keep a running list. You never know when you will need it for a minor character.

Male	Female

Character Descriptions from the Masters

From Harper Lee's *To Kill a Mockingbird* (1960):

"Calpurnia was something else again. She was all angles and bones; she was nearsighted; she squinted; her hand was wide as a bed slat and twice as hard. She was always ordering me out of the kitchen, asking me why I couldn't behave as well as Jem when she knew he was older, and calling me home when I wasn't ready to come. Our battles were epic and one-sided. Calpurnia always won, mainly because Atticus always took her side. She had been with us ever since Jem was born, and I had felt her tyrannical presence as long as I could remember."

From F. Scott Fitzgerald's *The Great Gatsby* (1925):

"He [Tom Buchanan] had changed since his New Haven years. Now he was a sturdy straw-haired man of thirty with a rather hard mouth and a supercilious manner. Two shining arrogant eyes had established dominance over his face and gave him the appearance of always leaning aggressively forward. Not even the effeminate swank of his riding clothes could hide the enormous power of that body — he seemed to fill those glistening boots until he strained the top lacing, and you could see a great pack of muscle shifting when his shoulder moved under his thin coat. It was a body capable of enormous leverage — a cruel body...His speaking voice, a gruff husky tenor, added to the impression of fractiousness he conveyed. There was a touch of paternal contempt in it, even toward people he liked..."

From Nathaniel Hawthorne's *The Scarlet Letter* (1850):

"The young woman [Hester Prynne] was tall, with a figure of perfect elegance on a large scale. She had dark and abundant hair, so glossy that it threw off the sunshine with a gleam; and a face which, besides being beautiful from regularity of feature and richness of complexion, had the impressiveness belonging to a marked brow and deep black eyes. She was ladylike, too, after the manner of the feminine gentility of those days; characterised by a certain state and dignity..."

"He was small in stature, with a furrowed visage, which as yet could hardly be termed aged. There was a remarkable intelligence in his features, as of a person who had so cultivated his mental part that it could not fail to mould the physical to itself and become manifest by unmistakable tokens. Although, by a seemingly careless arrangement of his heterogeneous garb, he had endeavoured to conceal or abate the peculiarity, it was sufficiently evident to Hester Prynne that one of this man's shoulders rose higher than the other. Again, at the first instant of perceiving that thin visage, and the slight deformity of the figure, she pressed her infant to her bosom with so convulsive a force that the poor babe uttered another cry."

From George Orwell's *1984* (1949):

"O'Brien was a large, burly man with a thick neck and a coarse, humorous, brutal face. In spite of his formidable appearance he had a certain charm of manner. He had a trick of resettling his spectacles on his nose which was curiously disarming—in some indefinable way, curiously civilized. It was a gesture which, if anyone had still thought in such terms, might have recalled an eighteenth-century nobleman offering his snuffbox."

"It was Mrs Parsons, the wife of a neighbour on the same floor... She was a woman of about thirty, but looking much older. One had the impression that there was dust in the creases of her face...She had a habit of breaking off her sentences in the middle...

NOTE: None of the above descriptions feel like a list.

Character Appearance Charts

Eye Color	Blue	Sky blue	Baby blue	Electric blue	Cornflower
	Brown	Chestnut	Chocolate	Cognac	Amber
	Green	Sea green	Moss green	Jade	Emerald
	Grey	Silver	Gunmetal grey	Charcoal	Black
	Hazel	Russet	Nut	Honey	Yellow
	Lavender	Other:			
Eye Shape	Almond	Round	Drooping	Hooded	Close-set
	Wide-set	Deep-set	Protruding	Sleepy	Squinting
	Down-turned	Other:			
Skin Tone	Fair	Ivory	Porcelain	Milk	Snow
	Ruddy	Rose	Peach	Ochre	Golden
	Olive	Khaki	Toffee	Honey	Tawny
	Dark	Ebony	Sepia	Russet	Mahogany
	Other:				
Body Shape	Triangle	Rectangle	Hourglass	Rounded	Diamond
	Inverted Triangle	Barrel	Willowy	Husky	Wiry
	Other:				
Facial Shapes	Oval	Rectangle	Square	Heart	Oblong
	Egg	Diamond	Triangle	Narrow	Block-like
	Other:				
Hair Color	Black	Dark brown	Medium brown	Ash brown	Golden brown
	Red	Auburn	Copper	Strawberry	Cinnamon
	Blond	Platinum	White	Silver	Grey
	Other:				
Notes:					

Considering World Population Percentages

When deciding on eye, hair, and skin tone, remember to keep in mind genetics and nationality. Not all of your characters should have green eyes since only two percent of the world population has that color. Do your research for the setting of your novel.

Eye Color	% of World Population
Brown	55-65% *Generally dominant
Blue	6-8% *Generally recessive
Hazel	5-8%
Amber	4-5%
Green	2% *Recessive, but dominant to blue
Silver/Grey	5% *Mostly Eastern European
Heterochromia	Less than 1%
Violet	Less than 1%
*Not all eye colors are included. Percentages are the averages found on Google searches.	

Dominant and Recessive Genetics

It turns out that the genetics I learned in Biology as a teenager are a little outdated. It *is* possible for two blue-eyed parents to have a brown-eyed child, though it is extremely rare. Two brown-eyed parents can indeed have a blue-eyed child if they each carry the blue gene. A recessive gene can stay hidden for generations, so don't stress about it too much; simply keep it in mind. It might be better to stick with traditional genetic traits. You don't want to distract your reader from the story with weird genetics, unless it is part of your plot.

Also, keep hair color on your radar. The majority of people in the world have black or dark brown hair. So, unless your story is about Vikings, make sure not everyone is blond.

Hair Color	% of World Population
Black to Dark Brown	70-80%
Medium to Light Brown	15-25%
Blonde	2-5% *highest % in Scandinavia
Red	1-2% *10% in the UK
*Not all hair colors are included. Percentages are the averages found on Google searches.	

One last thing about hair color: make sure you consider how you are going to spell everything. The word "brunette" is generally feminine. Also, in some countries, "blond" is male and "blonde" is female. Pick a style and be consistent.

Notes and Research on Character Traits

Figure out what unique traits your lead character is going to have, and do a little research. Make some notes and sketch a little if you like.

Character Comparison Chart

As you create your characters, keep a log of their general traits to make sure not too many characters end up with the same rare physical qualities. It can be helpful to see them in a grid for easy comparison.

Name	Eyes	Hair	Skin	Other

Name	Eyes	Hair	Skin	Other

Character Worksheet

Main Character: ☐ Protagonist ☐ Antagonist

	Name	Meaning
First		
Last		
Middle		

PHYSICAL DESCRIPTION

Gender:	Age:	Birthday:
Height:	Weight:	Body Shape:
Eye Color:	Eye Shape:	Lip Shape:
Face Shape:	Nose Shape:	Ear Shape:
Skin Tone:	Skin Texture:	Nationality:
Hair Color:	Hair Texture:	Voice:
Facial Expression/Physical Ticks/Other:		

INTERNAL DECRIPTION

Personality Type:	
Strengths/Talents/Powers/Skills:	
Flaws/Weaknesses/Limitations:	
Social Status:	Education:
Backstory: (Childhood, Romantic Relations, Philosophies, Etc.)	

Main Character: ☐ Protagonist ☐ Antagonist

	Name	Meaning
First		
Last		
Middle		

PHYSICAL DESCRIPTION

Gender:	Age:	Birthday:
Height:	Weight:	Body Shape:
Eye Color:	Eye Shape:	Lip Shape:
Face Shape:	Nose Shape:	Ear Shape:
Skin Tone:	Skin Texture:	Nationality:
Hair Color:	Hair Texture:	Voice:
Facial Expression/Physical Ticks/Other:		

INTERNAL DECRIPTION

<table>
<tr><td colspan="2">Personality Type:</td></tr>
<tr><td colspan="2">Strengths/Talents/Powers/Skills:</td></tr>
<tr><td colspan="2">Flaws/Weaknesses/Limitations:</td></tr>
<tr><td>Social Status:</td><td>Education:</td></tr>
<tr><td colspan="2">Backstory: (Childhood, Romantic Relations, Philosophies, Etc.)</td></tr>
</table>

Main Character: ☐ Protagonist ☐ Antagonist

	Name	Meaning
First		
Last		
Middle		

PHYSICAL DESCRIPTION

Gender:	Age:	Birthday:
Height:	Weight:	Body Shape:
Eye Color:	Eye Shape:	Lip Shape:
Face Shape:	Nose Shape:	Ear Shape:
Skin Tone:	Skin Texture:	Nationality:
Hair Color:	Hair Texture:	Voice:
Facial Expression/Physical Ticks/Other:		

INTERNAL DECRIPTION

Personality Type:	
Strengths/Talents/Powers/Skills:	
Flaws/Weaknesses/Limitations:	
Social Status:	Education:
Backstory: (Childhood, Romantic Relations, Philosophies, Etc.)	

Supporting Character: ☐ Sidekick ☐ Love Interest ☐ Mentor ☐ Fool ☐ Nemesis

	Name	Meaning
First		
Last		

PHYSICAL DESCRIPTION

Gender:	Age:	Height:
Eye Color:	Hair Color:	Weight & Body Shape:
Nationality:	Skin Tone:	Voice:
Facial Expression/Physical Ticks/Other:		

INTERNAL DECRIPTION

Personality Type:	
Strengths/Talents/Powers/Skills :	Flaws/Weaknesses/Limitations:
Backstory: (Why do we need this character?)	

Supporting Character: ☐ Sidekick ☐ Love Interest ☐ Mentor ☐ Fool ☐ Nemesis

	Name	Meaning
First		
Last		

PHYSICAL DESCRIPTION

Gender:	Age:	Height:
Eye Color:	Hair Color:	Weight & Body Shape:
Nationality:	Skin Tone:	Voice:
Facial Expression/Physical Ticks/Other:		

INTERNAL DECRIPTION:

Personality Type:	
Strengths/Talents/Powers/Skills:	Flaws/Weaknesses/Limitations:
Backstory: (Why do we need this character?)	

Supporting Character: ☐ Sidekick ☐ Love Interest ☐ Mentor ☐ Fool ☐ Nemesis

	Name	Meaning
First		
Last		

PHYSICAL DESCRIPTION

Gender:	Age:	Height:
Eye Color:	Hair Color:	Weight & Body Shape:
Nationality:	Skin Tone:	Voice:
Facial Expression/Physical Ticks/Other:		

INTERNAL DECRIPTION

Personality Type:	
Strengths/Talents/Powers/Skills :	Flaws/Weaknesses/Limitations:
Backstory: (Why do we need this character?)	

Supporting Character: ☐ Sidekick ☐ Love Interest ☐ Mentor ☐ Fool ☐ Nemesis

	Name	Meaning
First		
Last		

PHYSICAL DESCRIPTION

Gender:	Age:	Height:
Eye Color:	Hair Color:	Weight & Body Shape:
Nationality:	Skin Tone:	Voice:
Facial Expression/Physical Ticks/Other:		

INTERNAL DECRIPTION

Personality Type:	
Strengths/Talents/Powers/Skills:	Flaws/Weaknesses/Limitations:
Backstory: (Why do we need this character?)	

Supporting Character: ☐ Sidekick ☐ Love Interest ☐ Mentor ☐ Fool ☐ Nemesis

	Name	Meaning
First		
Last		

PHYSICAL DESCRIPTION

Gender:	Age:	Height:
Eye Color:	Hair Color:	Weight & Body Shape:
Nationality:	Skin Tone:	Voice:
Facial Expression/Physical Ticks/Other:		

INTERNAL DECRIPTION

Personality Type:	
Strengths/Talents/Powers/Skills :	Flaws/Weaknesses/Limitations:
Backstory: (Why do we need this character?)	

Supporting Character: ☐ Sidekick ☐ Love Interest ☐ Mentor ☐ Fool ☐ Nemesis

	Name	Meaning
First		
Last		

PHYSICAL DESCRIPTION

Gender:	Age:	Height:
Eye Color:	Hair Color:	Weight & Body Shape:
Nationality:	Skin Tone:	Voice:
Facial Expression/Physical Ticks/Other:		

INTERNAL DECRIPTION

Personality Type:	
Strengths/Talents/Powers/Skills :	Flaws/Weaknesses/Limitations:
Backstory: (Why do we need this character?)	

Emotions

Emotional Responses and Body Language

When you are writing, make sure that your characters have realistic emotional responses and body language. For example, if your protagonist is suffering from grief, have him or her go through the real life stages, even if it is accelerated.

Stages of Grief

Denial
Anger
Bargaining
Depression
Acceptance

If you are unsure how your character should react to a certain type of stimulus, hop online and do some research. There are tons of legitimate resources on the Internet. Doing research is part of writing, even if you are writing high fantasy. One of the comments I hear from my editor friends often is, "Do people seriously not know how to Google? Who in their right mind would [insert character reaction here]?"

What challenges your protagonist emotionally?

WHERE DO WE FEEL EMOTIONS?

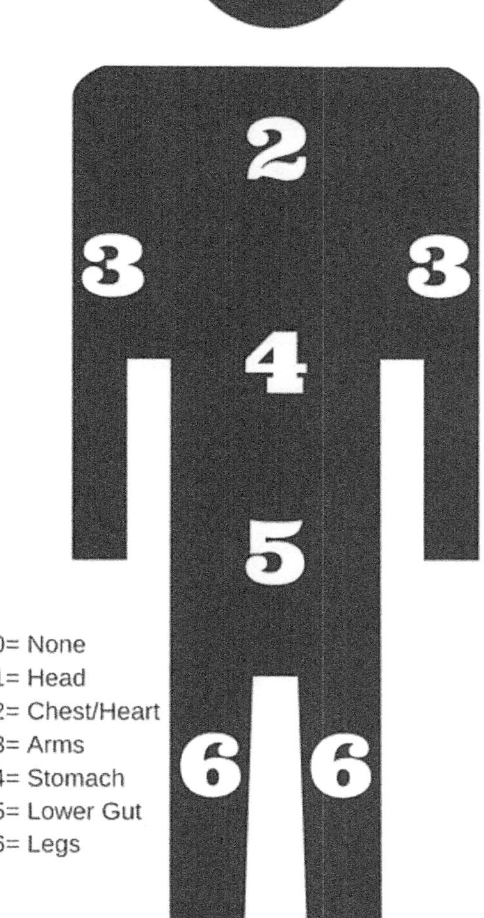

0= None
1= Head
2= Chest/Heart
3= Arms
4= Stomach
5= Lower Gut
6= Legs

	Response	
Emotion	Warm	Cool
Anger	1+, 2+, 3+	0
Anxiety	1, 2+, 4	6
Contempt	1	5
Depression	0	1, 3, 5, 6+
Disgust	1, 2, 4	5
Dread	1, 2	3, 5, 6
Envy	1, 2	5, 6
Fear	1, 2+, 4	0
Happiness	Full body	0
Love	Full body	0
Pride	1+, 2+, 3	0
Sadness	2-	3, 5, 6
Shame	1+, 2, 4	3, 5, 6
Surprise	1+, 2	6

+ indicates extra blood flow response in this area.

WRITE A PROPER REACTION: There is a known physiological response to different emotions, much of it having to do with how the heart and brain responds to different stimulus. If you are shocked or surprised, your heart beats faster pumping blood to places that need it. If a character is depressed, they are not going to have a warm response, but rather a cool response. Logically think through how your characters respond.

Research from pnas.org study and Cognative Therapy Sites

Your character just experienced something profoundly emotional. Write a paragraph or two about how the character physically reacts.

Dialogue

Tips on Dialogue

- **Every conversation should move the plot forward**. No empty fillers, please.
- **Don't overuse italics, ellipses, or exclamation points**.
- **There is no plot without conflict—you need conflict in your dialogue**.
- **Pick a punctuation style and stick to it**. If you are going to query a major publisher, you may want to use Chicago Manual of Style (CMOS). Regardless of what you choose to use, consistency is key. For example: if you use an en-dash when a character is cut off in a conversation, do it *every* time.
- **Avoid using the characters' names too much in dialogue**:

  "Hey, Eric."
  "Hello, Nora."
  "Eric, how has your summer been so far?"
  "Well, Nora, it has been rather busy. I'm ready to slow down for a bit."
  "I totally understand, Eric. I have been busy too."

  Besides the fact that the dialogue is a yawn fest, people don't naturally use one another's names *that* much in dialogue. This makes your characters sound like game show hosts.
- **Make sure not all of your characters sound the same**. Your adults should not sound like teenagers, teenagers should not sound like collegiate scholars, and someone from Alabama should not sound like they are from Oxford, England. Play with dialect and the way your characters use contractions.
- **Read it out loud or act it out**. This is the ultimate way to detect cheesy dialogue.
- **Too many perfect one-liners do not mean perfect**. Save them for when it counts—a handful in one book is plenty.
- **Generally, people don't speak in complete sentences**.

  "Would you like to go and get some coffee with me?"
  "I would love to go and get some coffee, but I don't have any money."
  "I have money, so it's my treat."

  "Coffee?"
  He gave her a doe-eyed look. "You buyin'?"
  Chuckling, she rolled her eyes while grabbing her wallet. "Let's go, mooch."
- **Restarts, stumbles, and stutters can improve emotional scenes**.

- **Silence can be powerful**. When people speak to one another, there are often long pauses in the conversation. Let your characters and audience digest heavy information by giving them the break to process it. It will not only highlight the information, but give it emotional weight. Here is a sample without the silence:

  "I'm dying," he stated.
  She swallowed. "How long?"
  "Three months."

  The above conversation lacks emotional depth. Adding silence can add the needed weight.

  "I'm dying." It was a simple statement . . . that changed everything.
  She sucked in a breath, but her eyes moved the lake. The wind caressed the water, sending glittering ripples into the distance. After a long while, she swallowed. "How long?"
  Before answering, he let out in a slow stream the breath he had been holding. "Three months."

- **Avoid too much description**. Unless your character is critiquing a piece of art, or analyzing something by pointing out details, don't have them say everything orally. I recently stopped reading a book because 95% of the character descriptions were in the dialogue. They were so long and awkward that they were unnatural, but also felt like a list. Below, I have written an example.

  He seductively pinned her to the wall, trailing his fingers across her jaw. She froze in fear as he leaned in even closer. His minty breath caused chills as he spoke, "My, what lovely eyes you have. They are such a unique color of blue—the specks of grey and whites almost make them look like the facets in a blue diamond. And your skin, it is so smooth I can't even see a pore on your face. It is the perfect balance of peaches 'n cream with a hint of olive. When I first saw you, I had expected your hair to feel different, but it is like fine, silken threads. It just makes me want to keep touching it. The color is mesmerizing, too. I can't decide if it is rich caramel or earthy amber. You are something, aren't you? You are the elixir I have been waiting for."

  Really? Who would speak like that in real life? If they did, we would think that they were strange and try to avoid them.

- **Obvious and parroting dialogue is boring—try a redirect.**

  "Hey, Jane. Awww, you look like you are having a bad day."
  "Yeah, I'm having a horrible day. It just won't end," Jane frowned.
  "The bad days always seem to go on and on, don't they?" Lisa sympathized.
  "Yes, they do. I can't wait until it is over."
  "Maybe we should go out for drinks after work?"
  "Drinks are a great idea!"
  "Are you free after work?"
  "Yes. In fact, drinking a lot of tequila sounds like a good plan."

  We read for heightened reality—not the mundane. Here is a sample of how to spruce up this dull conversation:

  Lisa came to a halt when she saw Jane. "Are you doing okay?"
  Jane pinned her brows together. "I need buckets of tequila to make this better."
  "Done. Meet me in the lobby at 5:00?"
  A wicked grin spread across Jane's face. "A cab will be waiting at the curb at 4:59."

  It still isn't perfect, but the same information was covered in half the lines.

Other tips you've discovered:

Write a short dialogue exchange using five of these tips to help transfer the knowledge into long-term memory.

Favorite Quotes

Keep a running list of quotes to use as an epigraph at the beginning of the novel.

There is nothing to writing. All you do is sit down at a typewriter and bleed.

--Ernest Hemingway

“

”

“ ds

”

Journal

Time to Write

Now that you have honed some of your skills, it is time to write. Remember the tent pole scenes you outlined earlier? Look those over and write them. Many of the most prolific and successful writers today write the end first. This helps you know where you are going. You may end up rewriting the scenes when you get to them, but having those scenes worked out will be invaluable.

You don't need to write every word of the chapter; just the meat of the scene. Use the next 25 pages to develop your climax, inciting incident, emotional epiphanies, etc.

Reference

Common Terms and Abbreviations in the Publishing World

As you delve into the publishing world, you will come across a whole new set of jargon that may seem foreign to you. Here is a quick reference list to help:

ARC = Advanced Reader Copy

ASIN = Amazon Standard Identification Number (An ISBN exclusively for Amazon)

Epigraph = A quote at the beginning of a book or chapter that usually sets the tone

Epilogue = A postscript that takes place after a novel or play and gives closure about the fates of the characters

MS = Manuscript

POV = Point of View

Prologue = An introductory scene that precedes the first scene of a novel or play

Proof = A physical copy of a book that is still being tweaked

RRP = Recommended Retail Price

WIP = Work in Progress

Did you know that most publishers in the U.S. use Chicago Style (CMOS)? Many writers use MLA or APA because that is what they used in university, but those styles are designed for the academic world.

Other Terms to Remember:

Rules of Using Numerals in Text

When writing numbers, it is sometimes tricky to figure out if you need to write 23 or twenty-three. I have compiled some rules that apply to almost all of the styles.

The General Rules

1. **Be consistent with your style.**

   Whether you write 1800's or 1800s, pick one and stick with it. See the rules of style for the guide in which you are following.

2. **Never begin a sentence with a numeral, spell it out.**

   8 criminals escaped during the prison transfer. ***Incorrect***.
   Eight criminals escaped during the prison transfer. ***Correct***.

   Though, it is often better to rephrase the sentence and not begin with a number.

3. **Spell out centuries and decades (unless you use the entire year).**

   Prohibition during the 20's strengthened organized crime. ***Incorrect.***
   The flappers of the Twenties were scandalous! ***Correct.***
   The eighteenth century was a time of change. ***Correct***.

4. **Spell out small numbers.**

   One monkey fell off the bed, leaving six uninjured monkeys.

5. **Hyphenate compound numbers from twenty-one to ninety-nine.**

   Twenty-two and fifty-one

6. **Don't mix numeral styles in a sentence.** (Yes, this may mean breaking another rule, but it is better to have that consistency thing we talked about earlier).
   I walk one mile a day, 14 times a month. ***Incorrect.***
   I walk one mile a day, fourteen times a month. ***Correct.***

7. **If you have numbers next to one another, spell one out for clarity.**

   The talent show had 8 8-year-olds perform during the assembly. ***Incorrect.***
   The talent show had 8 eight-year-olds perform during the assembly. ***Correct.***

8. **Use numerals for figures.**

   1.5 gallons or 9.2 liters
   48 days
   124 canisters

Samples:

- The plant grew five inches in a week.
- The company had to pay five million dollars in the settlement.
- The family lives at 808 Eight Street in a charming white house.
- The actress earned eight million dollars for her sixth film.
- Twenty-eight days after the accident, her cast was removed.
- John J. Loud patented the ballpoint pen on October 30, 1888. -OR- John J. Loud patented the ballpoint pen on 30 October 1888.

Other Notes:

Clichés to Avoid

Why should you avoid clichés? First, they are boring and lack imagination. You do not want to to appear like a lazy writer. But if you use a few, does that mean you are a terrible writer? No, but use them *very* sparingly and reword as much as you can. Second, clichés are vague and have often lost their meaning, so they are just fillers. Say what you mean. Be precise. Pick visual language.

- A baptism by fire
- A level playing field
- All walks of life
- At the end of the day
- Avoid like the plague
- Back on track
- Behind the eight ball
- Bitter end
- Calm before the storm
- Come full circle
- Cool as a cucumber
- Cry over spilled milk
- Easy come, easy go
- Every cloud has a silver lining
- Every rose has its thorn
- Fall on deaf ears
- Few and far between
- Give the devil his due
- Good things come to those who wait
- Hook, line, and sinker
- In the nick of time
- In the same boat
- In this day and age
- Leaps and bounds
- Leave no stone unturned
- Lock, stock, and barrel
- Long arm of the law
- March of history
- Mass exodus
- Never a dull moment
- Nipped in the bud
- Opposites attract
- Par for the course
- Patience of Job
- Paying the piper
- Sands of time
- The fact of the matter
- The path of least resistance
- Think outside the box
- To all intents and purposes
- When all is said and done
- Whirlwind tour
- Writing on the wall
- You win some, you lose some

Overused Clichés [in dialogue] from the Movies

Unfortunately, some great lines have been used in movies so often that they are now cringe-worthy in both print and film. [A greeting] "Well, if it isn't ___"

- "[Insert name] is my middle name."
- "All this and a paycheck too!"
- "Are you sitting down?"
- "Don't die on me."
- "Don't do anything stupid."
- "Get outta there!"
- "I could tell you, but then I would have to kill you."
- "I have a bad feeling about this."
- "I wouldn't do that if I were you."
- "I'm just doing my job."
- "I'm your worst nightmare."
- "If you touch one hair on his/her head…"
- "If you're on time, you're late."
- "Is that all you've got?"
- "Is this some kind of sick joke?"
- "It's called ___, you should try it sometime."
- "It's gonna blow!"
- "It's just a scratch."
- "It's not what it looks like."
- "Not on my watch."
- "Now, where were we?"
- "She/He's behind me, isn't she/he?"
- "Shut up and kiss me."
- "Sit down and shut up."
- "Speak of the devil."
- "Tell [insert name] that I love him/her."
- "That's the pot calling the kettle black."
- "There's a storm coming."
- "This ain't my first rodeo, cowboy."
- "This is your destiny." Or "This is why you were born."
- "This just gets better and better."
- "We can do this the easy way, or the hard way."
- "We'll never make it in time!"
- "We're not so different, you and I."
- "We're putting on another dog and pony show."
- "We've got company!"
- "We've got to stop meeting like this."
- "What just happened?"
- "What part of ___ don't you understand?"
- "Whatever you do, don't look down."
- "Yeah, you better run!"
- "You and what army?"
- "You just don't get it, do you?"
- "You look like shit."
- "You say that like it's a bad thing."
- "You'll never get away with this!"

Newbie Errors

"Amateurs sit and wait for inspiration, the rest of us just get up and go to work."
— Stephen King, *On Writing: A Memoir of the Craft*

These are in no particular order; they are simply things that I see new and self-published authors doing, which makes their work less professional. Honestly, it comes down to editing. Most new writers don't want to spend money on having their work professionally edited, but it is imperative.

Be consistent. Pick a style and stick to it. This goes for everything from the way you use contractions to punctuation to dialogue tags.

Use the Oxford Comma in works of fiction. There is some debate on this, but in longer works of fiction, it is generally preferred.

Use "all right" and not "alright." Unless you are using obvious slang in some dialogue, like "alrighty", avoid using this. "Alright" may have been added into urban dictionaries, but so has the word "literally" under the word "figuratively." Look like a pro and spell it right.

A lot means "many." Whereas, alot means nothing, since it isn't actually a word.

Pick a font that has curved quotation marks. "This" and not "this." It may seem random, but the pros will scoff at you. If you fall in love with a font that has straight quote marks, it is possible to change it in the options/setting if you are tech savvy.

Use a font with serifs, as opposed to a "sans serif" like Ariel. It doesn't need to be Times New Roman, but something in that family. Fonts with serifs are easier to read in print, whereas sans serifs are better on screens. Therefore, you may want to use serifs for the hard copy, and san serifs for the eBook.

Overly long sentences or paragraphs. Give your readers a break by visually breaking up your words. People who read for pleasure don't want to feel taxed by reading.

The BIGGEST newbie mistake? Not having your MS professionally edited. You need to go through your MS several times and clean it up BEFORE handing your precious baby over to someone else. Have friends with good grammar skills go through it too. But always have a pro do it. Make sure you find an editor who is a good fit.

Avoid Language that Offends

Sometimes we don't think about the language we have grown up hearing. Try to avoid language that is belittling. Of course, if you have a sexist or racist character, use it in their dialogue.

Samples of Sexist, Discriminatory, and Stereotypical Language

Original	Alternate
Authoress	Author
Chairman, chairwoman	Chairperson, person, coordinator
Common man	Ordinary people, average person
Congressman	Congressional representative, legislator
Fireman	Firefighter
Housewife	Homemaker
Invalid	Disabled
Mailman	Mail carrier, postal worker
Male nurse	Nurse
Mankind	Humanity, human race, human beings, people
Man-made	Manufactured, synthetic
Policewoman, policeman	Police officer
Six man-hours	Six working-hours, six staff-hours
Stewardess, steward	Flight attendant
To man	To staff, to operate
Weatherman	Meteorologist, forecaster
Workman	Worker, laborer
Notes:	

Number Symbolism

In literature, you often see repetitions of certain numbers. How many little pigs were there? How many blind mice? Choosing numbers that have symbolic meaning and weight can add depth to your narrative.

Popular Symbolic Numbers	
Two	Duality, partnership, male & female, yin & yang, left & right, hot & cold, sun & moon, night & day, active & passive, other:
Three	Trinity (Father, Son, & Holy Spirit), circle of life (birth, life, & death), idea of self (mind, body, & spirit), mystical number in folktales (three wishes, three challenges, three guesses, etc.), three rulers in Greek mythology (Zeus, Hades, & Poseidon), three Fates, Shakespeare's *Macbeth* has three witches, other:
Four	Four elements (earth, air, wind, & fire), four cardinal points (north, south, east, & west), humanity (four limbs), four seasons, four humors (blood, choler, phlegm, & black bile), four phases of the moon, four horseman of the Apocalypse, other:
Six	Satan, evil, the devil, other:
Seven	Trinity plus humanity (3+4), days of the week, seven deadly sins, other:
Nine	Nine lives of a cat, Norse mythology there are nine worlds, Greek mythology there are nine Muses, other:
Twelve	A complete cycle, Twelve months, twelve hours, twelve disciples of Christ, twelve tribes of Israel, twelve inches in a foot, other:
Thirteen	Unlucky, bad luck, Judas was the thirteenth person to arrive to the last supper, other:
Forty	Trials and tribulations, Hebrews wandered for forty years , other:
Notes:	

Symbolism of Flowers

Adding Depth to Writing and Understanding. I have gathered meanings and symbolism over the years and compiled them on this list. Most of the meanings listed are from older texts, especially from the Victorian Era. Thus, some of the meanings have changed in recent years (I blame the florists), but I stick with the older meanings.

Flower/Plant	Meaning
Amaryllis	Immortality, unfading love
Apple Blossoms	Preference
Azalea	Temperance (self-control)
Bluebell	Constancy
Camellia	Red - Loveliness; White - Excellence
Carnation	Pink - A woman's love; Red - Alas my poor heart, Striped - Refusal; Yellow - Disdain
Chrysanthemum	Red - Love; Yellow - Slighted love; White – Truth
Daffodil	Regard; Yellow - Chivalry
Daisy	Innocence, I will think on it
Fern	Fascination
Gladiolus	Strength of character
Grass	Usefulness
Heather	Solitude (being alone)
Ivy	Friendship, fidelity (faithfulness)
Jasmine	Grace, elegance
Lavender	Distrust
Lilac	First emotions of love
Lily	Sweetness, purity
Magnolia	Dignity
Myrtle	Love
Narcissus	Arrogance, egotism
Rose	Red - Love; White - Purity; Burgundy – Beauty, Yellow - Decrease of love, infidelity
Rosemary	Remembrance
Rue	Disdain
Sunflower	Haughtiness (pride)
Tulip	Love
Wisteria	I cling to thee

Other Symbols

Tastes and Aromas

When you are writing, try to incorporate all four of the senses in your work. Here is a cheat sheet for tastes and smells:

Positive	Neutral	Negative	Spices	Florals (Most Fragrant)
Aromatic	Acidic	Biting	Cajun	Angel's Trumpet
Citrusy	Acrid	Bitter	Cinnamon	Flowering Plum
Comforting	Airy	Decay	Clove	Heliotrope
Crisp	Ancient	Dirty	Coriander	Honeysuckle
Exquisite	Brackish	Fetid	Cumin	Jasmin
Fragrant	Burnt	Foul	Pepper	Lilac
Fresh	Delicate	Funky	Sage	Mexican Orange
Fruity	Feminine	Gamy	Thyme	Mock Orange
Full-bodied	Fermented	Harsh	Basil	Rose
Hard	Masculine	Moldy	Barbeque	Star Magnolia
Heady	Floral	Musty	Bay Leaf	Sweet Peas
Juicy	Humid	Nasty	Curry	Tuberose
Lemony	Light	Noxious	Anise	
Rich	Medicinal	Old	Caraway Seed	Household Smells
Savory	Medium	Pungent	Cardamom	
Sharp	Mellow	Putrid	Cayenne	Babies
Succulent	Metallic	Rancid	Dill	"Boy" Smell
Sugary	Mild	Rank	Fennel	Bacon
Sweet	Minty	Repulsive	Garlic	BBQ
Tangy	Moist	Rotting	Ginger	Beer
Tart	Musky	Skunky	Mace	Books
Tempting	Nippy	Sour	Marjoram	Bread
Warm	Nutty	Spoiled	Mustard	Burning Wood
Woody	Peppery	Stagnant	Onion	Chocolate
Zesty	Perfumed	Stench	Orange Peel	Cinnamon
Zingy	Salty	Stinking	Lemon Peel	Citrus
	Woodsy	Stuffy	Nutmeg	Coconut
Other:	Yeasty		Rosemary	Coffee
		Other:	Saffron	Cut Grass
	Other:		Turmeric	Dirty Laundry
			Vanilla	Fresh–baked cookies
				Fresh Laundry
				Pine
				Soap

100 Power Words to Know and Use

Adversary	Habitation	Replenish
Aplomb	Hasten	Repugnant
Apprehensive	Headway	Restitution
Aptitude	Ignite	Sabotage
Attentive	Illuminate	Serenity
Banish	Impending	Sociable
Barricade	Imperious	Somber
Bluff	Jabber	Specimen
Brackish	Jargon	Stamina
Brandish	Jostle	Subside
Circumference	Jut	Swagger
Commotion	Kindle	Swarm
Concoction	Knoll	Tactic
Conspicuous	Luminous	Terse
Contortion	Malleable	Translucent
Counter	Materialize	Uncanny
Cunning	Meander	Unsightly
Debris	Meticulous	Versatile
Defiance	Misgiving	Vigilant
Deft	Momentum	Vulnerable
Destination	Monotonous	Waft
Diminish	Multitude	Waver
Disdain	Muster	Weather
Dismal	Narrate	Zeal
Dispel	Obscure	
Eavesdrop	Ominous	Notes
Egregious	Outlandish	
Ember	Persistent	
Emerge	Pertinent	
Engross	Plenteous	
Exasperation	Potential	
Exhilarate	Precipice	
Falter	Pristine	
Foresight	Quell	
Fragrance	Recluse	
Furtive	Recuperate	
Grueling	Scarcity	
Gusto	Scurry	

Darkness & Light

LIGHT
Ablaze
Alabaster
Amber
Ambient
Angled
Blanched
Blazing
Bleached
Bluish
Bright
Brilliant
Bubbling
Burning
Burnished
Chalky
Clear
Cold
Cool
Crystalline
Curved
Dancing
Dim
Distant
Effervescent
Filtered
Frosted
Ghostly
Gilded
Glaring
Glittering
Glossy
Glowing
Golden
Harsh
Igniting
Ivory
Kindling
Lustrous

LIGHT CONT.
Milky
Murky
Opaque
Pulsing
Refracting
Shiny
Slithering
Soft
Sparkling
Spiraling
Splintered
Spotlighting
Straight
Sunny
Thick
Thin
Wan
Warm
White

PHYSICAL TYPES
Direct
Indirect
Backlight

Artificial
Halogen
Fluorescent
Incandescent
Iridescent
LED
Phosphorescence

Natural
Firelight
Moonlight
Sunlight

FEELINGS ASSOCIATED
All-encompassing
Appealing
Beckoning
Confining
Constraining
Controlling
Dismal
Fierce
Forgiving
Forlorn
Freeing
Frightening
Glorious
Growing
Heavy
Intense
Joyous
Light
Lonely
Menacing
Mesmerizing
Oppressive
Playful
Radiating
Relentless
Searching
Secluding
Secretive
Smothering
Somber
Terrible
Terrifying
Threatening
Whimsical
Yawning
Yearning

DARKNESS
Black
Clouded
Concentrated
Corrupting
Diabolical
Dingy
Drab
Dull
Ebony
Foul
Gloomy
Grimy
Impure
Ink-like
Inky
Jet
Lurid
Misty
Malevolent
Mournful
Nebulous
Obscure
Obsidian
Onyx
Oppressive
Pitch
Raven
Shadowy
Shady
Slate
Sooty
Squalid
Starless
Stubborn
Sullen
Villainous
Wicked

Thoughts on Writing from the Masters

“Substitute 'damn' every time you're inclined to write 'very;' your editor will delete it and the writing will be just as it should be.” — **Mark Twain**

“One day I will find the right words, and they will be simple.”
— **Jack Kerouac**, ***The Dharma Bums***

“And by the way, everything in life is writable about if you have the outgoing guts to do it, and the imagination to improvise. The worst enemy to creativity is self-doubt.”
— **Sylvia Plath**, ***The Unabridged Journals of Sylvia Plath***

“No tears in the writer, no tears in the reader. No surprise in the writer, no surprise in the reader.” — **Robert Frost**

“Read, read, read. Read everything—trash, classics, good and bad, and see how they do it. Just like a carpenter who works as an apprentice and studies the master. Read! You'll absorb it. Then write. If it's good, you'll find out. If it's not, throw it out of the window.”
— **William Faulkner**

“You must stay drunk on writing so reality cannot destroy you.”
— **Ray Bradbury**, ***Zen in the Art of Writing***

“The road to hell is paved with adverbs.” — **Stephen King**, ***On Writing***

“Don't tell me the moon is shining; show me the glint of light on broken glass.”
— **Anton Chekhov**

“Start writing, no matter what. The water does not flow until the faucet is turned on.”
— **Louis L'Amour**

“The first draft of anything is shit.” — **Ernest Hemingway**

“This is how you do it: you sit down at the keyboard and you put one word after another until its done. It's that easy, and that hard.” — **Neil Gaiman**

“You can't wait for inspiration. You have to go after it with a club.” — **Jack London**

“Write the kind of story you would like to read. People will give you all sorts of advice about writing, but if you are not writing something you like, no one else will like it either.”
— **Meg Cabot**

“Cut out all these exclamation points. An exclamation point is like laughing at your own joke.” — **F. Scott Fitzgerald**

Synonyms

As you are editing, it is important to pay attention to repetition. Much of the tinkering with words will come with editing, but I love using synonym sheets to cut down on the editing later, as well as to inspire me.

Emotions

Other words for Happy

Alluring, amused, appealing, appeased, blissful, blithe, carefree, charmed, cheeky, chipper, chirpy, content, convivial, delighted, elated, electrified, ecstatic, enchanted, enthusiastic, exultant, excited, fantastic, fulfilled, glad, gleeful, glowing, gratified, idyllic, intoxicating, jolly, joyful, joyous, jovial, jubilant, light, lively, merry, mirthful, overjoyed, pleased, pleasant, radiant, sparkling, savoured, satisfied, serene, sunny, thrilled, tickled, up, upbeat, winsome, wonderful.

Other words for SAD

Aching, agitated, anguished, anxious, bleak, bothered, brooding, bugged, chagrined, cheerless, darkly, disillusioned, disappointed, disenchanted, disheartened, dismayed, distraught, dissatisfied, despondent, doleful, failed, faint, frustrated, glazed, gloomy, glowering, haunted, hopeless, languid, miserable, pained, perturbed, sour, suffering, sullen, thwarted, tormented, troubled, uneasy, unsettled, upset, vacant, vexed, wan, woeful, wounded.

Other words for Mad

Affronted, aggravated, agitated, angered, annoyed, bitter, boiling, bothered, brooding, bugged, bummed, cantankerous, chafed, chagrined, crabby, cross, disgruntled, distraught, disturbed, enflamed, enraged, exasperated, fiery, fuming, furious, frantic, galled, goaded, hacked, heated, hostile, hot, huffy, ill-tempered, incensed, indignant, inflamed, infuriated, irate, ireful, irritated, livid, maddened, malcontent, miffed, nettled, offended, peeved, piqued, provoked, raging, resentful, riled, scowling, sore, sour, stung, taut, tense, tight, troubled, upset, vexed, wrathful.

Other words for Crying

Bawling, blubbering, gushing, howling, lamenting, moaning, scream-crying, silent tears, sniffling, snivelling, sobbing, sorrowing, teary, wailing, weepy, woeful.

Commonly Used Words

Other words for ASKED

Appealed, begged, beckoned, beseeched, besieged, bid, craved, commanded, claimed, coaxed, challenged, charged, charmed, cross-examined, demanded, drilled, entreated, enchanted, grilled, implored, imposed, interrogated, invited, invoked, inquired, insisted, needled, ordered, pleaded, petitioned, picked, probed, pried, pressed, pumped, pursued, put through the wringer, put the screws down, questioned, queried, quizzed, requested, required, requisitioned, roasted, solicited, summoned, surveyed, sweated, urged, wanted, wheedled, wooed, worried, wondered.

Other words for LAUGH

Break up, burst, cackle, chortle, chuckle, crack-up, crow, giggle, grin, guffaw, hee-haw, howl, peal, quack, roar, scream, shriek, snicker, snigger, snort, split one's sides, tee-hee, titter, whoop.

Other Words for LOOK

Address, admire, attention, audit, babysit, beam, beholding, blink, bore, browse, burn, cast, check, comb, consider, contemplate, delve, detect, discover, disregard, distinguish, ensure, evil eye, examine, explore, eye, eyeball, ferret, fix, flash, forage, gander, gaze, get an eyeful, give the eye, glance, glare, glaze, glimmer, glimpse, glitter, gloat, goggle, grope, gun, have a gander, inquire, inspect, investigate, judge, keeping watch, leaf-through, leer, lock daggers on, look fixedly, look-see, marking, moon, mope, neglect, note, notice, noting, observe, ogle, once-over, peek, peep, peer, peg, peruse, poke into, scan, pout, probe, pry, quest, rake, recognize, reconnaissance, regard, regarding, renew, resemble, review, riffle, rubberneck, rummage, scan, scowl, scrutinize, search, seeing, sense, settle, shine, sift, simper, size-up, skim, slant, smile, smirk, snatch, sneer, speculative, spot, spy, squint, stare, study, sulk, supervise, surveillance, survey, sweep, take stock of, take in, trace, verify, view, viewing, watch, witness, yawp, zero in.

Other words for REPLIED

Acknowledged, answered, argued, accounted, barked, bit, be in touch, boomeranged, comeback, countered, conferred, claimed, denied, echoed, feedback, fielded the question, get back to, growled, matched, parried, reacted, reciprocated, rejoined, responded, retorted, remarked, returned, retaliated, shot back, snapped, squelched, squared, swung, vacillated.

Other words for **Sat**

Be seated, bear on, cover, ensconce, give feet a rest, grab a chair, have a place, have a seat, hunker, install, lie, park, perch, plop down, pose, posture, put it there, relax, remain, rest, seat, seat oneself, settle, squat, take a load off, take a place, take a seat.

Other words for **Was/Were** VERB (TO BE)

Abided, acted, be alive, befell, breathed, continued, coexisted, do, endured, ensued, existed, had been, happened, inhabited, lasted, lived, moved, obtained, occurred, persisted, prevailed, remained, rested, stood, stayed, survived, subsided, subsisted, transpired.

Other words for **Walk**

Advance, amble, barge, bolt, bounce, bound, canter, charge, crawl, creep, dance, dash, escort, gallop, hike, hobble, hop, jog, jump, leap, limp, lope, lumber, meander, mosey, move, pad, pace march, parade, patrol, plod, prance, proceed, promenade, prowl, race, roam, rove, run, sashay, saunter, scamper, scramble, zip shuffle, skip, slink, slither, slog, sprint, stagger, step, stomp, stride, stroll, strut, stumble, swagger, thread, tiptoe, traipse, tramp, tread, trek, trip, trot, trudge, wade, wander.

Other words for **Whisper**

Breathed, buzz, disclosed, exhaled, expressed, fluttered, gasped, hint, hiss, hum, hushed tone, intoned, lament, low voice, moaned, mouthed, mumble, murmur, mutter, puff, purred, reflected, ruffle, rumble, rush, said low, said softly, sigh, sob, undertone, utter, voiced, wheezed.

Other words for **Went**

Abscond, ambled, approached, avoided, be off, beat it, bolted, bounced, bounded, bugged out, burst, carved, cleared out, crawled, crept, cruised, cut and run, danced, darted, dashed, decamped, deserted, disappeared, ducked out, escaped, evaded, exited, fared, fled, floated, flew, flew the coop, galloped, got away, got going, got lost, glided, go down. go south, hightailed, hit the road, hoofed it, hopped, hotfooted, hurdled, hustled, journeyed, jumped, leapt, left, lighted out, loped, lunged, made haste, made a break for it, made for, made off, made tracks, marched, moseyed, moved, muscled, neared, negotiated, paced, paraded, passed, pedalled, proceeded, progressed, pulled out, pulled, pushed off, pushed on, quitted, retired, retreated, rode, ran along, ran away, rushed, sashayed, scampered, scooted, scrammed, scurried, scuttled, set off, set out, shot, shouldered, shoved off, shuffled, skedaddled, skipped out, skipped, skirted, slinked, slipped, soared, split, sprang, sprinted, stole away, steered clear, stepped on it, strolled, strutted, scurried, swept, took a hike, took a powder, took flight, took leave, took off, threaded, toddled, tottered, trampled, travelled, traversed, trekked, trode, trudged, tumbled, vamoosed, vanished, vaulted, veered, walked off, wandered, weaved, wended, whisked, withdrew, wormed, zipped, zoomed.

Other words for SAID

accused, acknowledged, added, announced, addressed, admitted, advised, affirmed, agreed, asked, avowed, asserted, answered, apologized, argued, assured, approved, articulated, alleged, attested, barked, bet, bellowed, babbled, begged, bragged, began, bawled, bleated, blurted, boomed, broke in, bugged, boasted, bubbled, beamed, burst out, believed, brought out, confided, crowed, coughed, cried, congratulated, complained, conceded, chorused, concluded, confessed, chatted, convinced, chattered, cheered, chided, chimed in, clucked, coaxed, commanded, cautioned, continued, commented, called, croaked, chuckled, claimed, choked, chortled, corrected, communicated, claimed, contended, criticized, construe,

dared, decided, disagreed, described, disclosed, drawled, denied, declared, demanded, divulged, doubted, denied, disputed, dictated, echoed, ended, exclaimed, explained, expressed, enunciated, expounded, emphasized, formulated, fretted, finished, gulped, gurgled, gasped, grumbled, groaned, guessed, gibed, giggled, greeted, growled, grunted, hinted, hissed, hollered, hypothesized, inquired, imitated, implied, insisted, interjected, interrupted, intoned, informed, interpreted, illustrated, insinuated, jeered, jested, joked, justified, lied, laughed, lisped, maintained, muttered, marveled, moaned, mimicked, mumble, modulated, murmured, mused, mentioned, mouthed, nagged, noted, nodded, noticed,

objected, observed, offered, ordered, owned up, piped, pointed out, panted, pondered, praised, prayed, puzzled, proclaimed, promised, proposed, protested, purred, pled, pleaded, put in, prevailed, parried, pressed, put forward, pronounced, pointed out, prescribed, popped off, persisted, protested, questioned, quavered, quipped, quoted, queried, rejected, reasoned, ranted, reassured, reminded, responded, recalled, returned, requested, roared, related, remarked, replied, reported, revealed, rebutted, retorted, repeated, reckoned, remembered, regarded, recited, resolved, reflected, ripped, rectified, reaffirmed,

snickered, sniffed, smirked, snapped, snarled, shot, sneered, sneezed, started, stated, stormed, sobbed, stuttered, suggested, surmised, sassed, sputtered, sniffled, snorted, spoke, stammered, squeaked, sassed, scoffed, scolded, screamed, shouted, sighed, smiled, sang, shrieked, shrilled, speculated, supposed, settled, solved, shot back, swore, stressed, spilled, told, tested, trilled, taunted, teased, tempted, theorized, threatened, tore, uttered, unveiled, urged, upheld, vocalized, voiced, vindicated, volunteered, vowed, vented, verbalized, warned, wailed, went on, wept, whimpered, whined, wondered, whispered, worried, warranted, yawned, yakked.

My Synonym Lists:

My Synonym Lists:

Post First Draft

Self-Editing Checklist

I have adapted this list from a great self-editing article written by Tamar Hela (who has given me permission to use it).

This checklist is simple and straightforward:

1. **Check spelling**—don't rely on spell check for everything, either!

2. **Check grammar**—word processors only catch a fraction of the errors.

3. **Proofread your writing *at least* THREE TIMES**—don't be lazy!

4. **Review the context/meaning of your wording.**
   -Did you use the right words?
   -Do you have misplaced/dangling modifiers?
   -Is your message clear and concise?
   -Did you cut/edit unnecessary wording?

5. **Check your dates and times** (as applicable).
   -Calendar dates accurate?
   -Does a sunset or sunrise happen at the correct time for the season?
   -Did your characters have enough time to travel? Search actual travel times.
   -Are your emotional recover times true to life?

6. **Check your sources** (as applicable).

7. **If working in a Word/Pages document, save often.**

8. **Do you have permission to use the quotes from other authors?** (as applicable)
   -If the work is in the public domain, quote away.
   -The Gutenberg Project provides free public domain works.
   -Contact publishers to purchase the rights, or use something pre-1900.

If you are sending the MS to an editor, make sure you follow their format guidelines. Also, spend some time vetting your editors. Don't waste money hiring someone who is unprofessional or not up to par with industry standards.

Beta Readers

I have a team of beta readers go through my novels after my editors have gone through them. I think of it as a gauntlet of sorts, and I usually feel pretty beat up after the process is over, but I am the better for it.

When choosing beta readers, I make sure that I pick people (both male and female) who are avid readers, but have diverse backgrounds. I try to have English teachers, as well as engineers, read through my MS. The math/science person will question your facts and figures, while the English/humanities person will weigh your grammar and emotional content.

Note: Unless you manage to land one of the big five publishers, you need to make sure your book is well-edited. Yes, *you*—don't be lazy. And anyone who tells you that the editing doesn't make a difference is just wrong.

On my third novel, I started inviting my beta readers to a Google doc. This allowed me to keep up with edits in real time, and it cut down on the amount of repeat comments I had. I was also able to ask clarifying questions. This is how I set up my document: (These are real edits for *The Fallen: Part One.* My replies are in italics)

Pg	Error	Fix/Comment	Fixed
9	5th para, "after being roughly"	her head or all of her?	✔
10	2nd to last paragraph: set of stairs… set of doors ("set" twice in a row)	Change if you want--not a huge deal, though IMHO *Changed first to staircase*	✔
11	5th para, "wanted me dead and"	needs comma before and	✔
33	Middle, "200"	Why is this not written out? *Reference to the Apocrypha--I kept it in the same format*	X

I have my readers color-code their comments so I know who I am responding to. I mark the right column with accepted or rejected comments.

Social Media

It is never too early to start building your social media presence. I do have a few tips for you, though. Many of them I learned the hard way.

1. **BRAND YOURSELF, not your book**. You may decide to write another book, and it might be in a different genre. If you brand yourself, it gives you lots of flexibility.

2. **Build relationships with other authors, as well as potential fans**. Think of other authors as teammates, not competition. When people like a certain type of book, they want to read more like it. There is no need to undercut others. If you build allies, you will be amazed at how much they will help you. Be generous.

3. **Take advantage of free resources**. It is tempting to go out and purchase all sorts of services. Use the free versions for at least a few months before paying. You will find what you do and do not use. If you start early, you will have plenty of time before you need to launch a full-scale author page.

3. **Don't spend more than 10-15% of your time on social media**. You need to guard your writing (and editing) time. Don't allow distraction to become your nemesis.

4. **Don't make it all about you**. If everything is a sales pitch, people will mute you.

5. **Focus on three or four services,** and do them well. I spend my time on Twitter, Pinterest, and Facebook. But things are changing all the time. Once a venue is no longer relevant, move on and find one that is.

6. **Proofread everything you post, even tweets**. You are human. An occasional typo is fine, but try to avoid them.

Other Research

Books by Robin Woods

Available on Amazon

Fiction Books: The Watcher Series

Allure: A Watcher Series Prequel
The Unintended: Book One
The Nexus: Book Two
The Sacrifice: Book Three
The Fallen Part One: Book Four
The Fallen Part Two: Book Five

Non-Fiction: Creative Writing Books

Prompt Me Novel: Workbook & Journal
Prompt Me Workbook & Journal
Prompt Me More: Workbook & Journal
Prompt Me Again: Workbook & Journal
Prompt Me Romance: Workbook & Journal
Prompt Me Sci-Fi & Fantasy: Workbook
Prompt Me Horror & Thriller: Workbook

Picture This Photo Prompts & Inspiration (Full-color, digital spin-off available on Kindle)
Prompt Me Reading Log & Analysis (Easy way to log reading chapter-by-chapter)

Coming in 2020:

Prompt Me Mystery & Suspense and *Light & Shadow: Watcher Series Shorts & Extras*

About the Author

Robin Woods is a former high school and university instructor with two and a half decades of experience teaching English, literature, and writing. She has earned a BA in English and an MA in Education.

In addition to teaching, Robin Woods has published six highly-rated novels and has multiple projects in the works.

When Ms. Woods isn't writing, she is chasing her two elementary school kids around and spending time with her ever-patient husband.

For more information and free resources, go to her website at:

Thank you for reading. If you enjoyed this book, please take a moment to write a review. It is the best way to help the authors you love. Books without reviews simply don't sell and your support is critical. Reviews don't have to be long.

Something as simple as:

I liked ___ and ___. I would recommend it to ___.

Thank you so much. Blessings!

Made in the USA
Las Vegas, NV
29 April 2025